RECITAL REPERTOIRE FOR CELLISTS

Selected and edited by Julian Lloyd Webber and Simon Nicholls
for Cello and Piano · Book Two

Faber Music Limited

London

Preface

The 12 pieces included in the two volumes of *Recital Repertoire for Cellists* follow on naturally from *The Young Cellist's Repertoire* Book 3. Now the emphasis is on performance, and we hope that in addition to their value for teaching, these works may prove useful as alternatives to more traditional recital material.

Once again, a wide variety of styles is represented in each volume, ranging from the Baroque era to the 20th century, and the selection has been made as much for musical as for technical content. We are particularly pleased to include the Scherzetto by Frank Bridge, which is published here for the first time.

Wherever possible the text is based on original sources, but the realisations from figured bass and the fingerings and bowings in the solo part are the responsibility of the editors.

JULIAN LLOYD WEBBER

SIMON NICHOLLS

The Bridge Scherzetto is also available on hire from the publishers in an arrangement for cello and orchestra by Robert Cornford

© 1987 by Faber Music Ltd
First published in 1987 by Faber Music Ltd
3 Queen Square London WC1N 3AU
Music engraved by Allan Hill
Cover design by Ian Chilvers
Printed in England by Halstan & Co. Ltd

Contents

1. Bohemian Dance

Simon Nicholls

2. Prelude

Alexander Skryabin, arr. S.N.
(1872–1915)

3. Finnländisch

Max Bruch
(1838–1920)

4. Adagio and Allegro

(from Sonata in F)

Pasqualino de Marzis
(fl. c1730–45)

5. Lied ohne Worte
(Song without Words)

Felix Mendelssohn, arr. S.N.
(1809–1847)

6. Scherzetto

Frank Bridge
(1879–1941)

---

* The upbeats to bs. 3, 22, 98 and 117 are slurred into the
following note in Bridge's MS

** At bs. 58 and 66 the slur continues over the barline in the MS

RECITAL REPERTOIRE FOR CELLISTS

Selected and edited by Julian Lloyd Webber and Simon Nicholls
for Cello and Piano · Book Two

Faber Music Limited
London

Preface

The 12 pieces included in the two volumes of *Recital Repertoire for Cellists* follow on naturally from *The Young Cellist's Repertoire* Book 3. Now the emphasis is on performance, and we hope that in addition to their value for teaching, these works may prove useful as alternatives to more traditional recital material.

Once again, a wide variety of styles is represented in each volume, ranging from the Baroque era to the 20th century, and the selection has been made as much for musical as for technical content. We are particularly pleased to include the Scherzetto by Frank Bridge, which is published here for the first time.

Wherever possible the text is based on original sources, but the realisations from figured bass and the fingerings and bowings in the solo part are the responsibility of the editors.

JULIAN LLOYD WEBBER

SIMON NICHOLLS

The Bridge Scherzetto is also available on hire from the publishers
in an arrangement for cello and orchestra by Robert Cornford

© 1987 by Faber Music Ltd
First published in 1987 by Faber Music Ltd
3 Queen Square London WC1N 3AU
Music engraved by Allan Hill
Cover design by Ian Chilvers
Printed in England by Halstan & Co. Ltd

Contents

1. Bohemian Dance

Simon Nicholls

2. Prelude

Alexander Skryabin, arr. S.N.
(1872–1915)

3. Finnländisch

Max Bruch
(1838–1920)

4. Adagio and Allegro

(from Sonata in F)

Pasqualino de Marzis, realised S.N.
(fl. c1730–45)

5. Lied ohne Worte
(Song without Words)

Felix Mendelssohn, arr. S.N.
(1809–1847)

6. Scherzetto

Frank Bridge
(1879–1941)

* The upbeats to bs. 3, 22, 98 and 117 are slurred into the
following note in Bridge's MS

18

* At bs. 58 and 66 the slur continues over the barline in the MS